Robo-Recruiting: Building an AI-Powered Staffing and HR Consultancy

By Silas Meadowlark

Index

- The Rise of AI in Talent Acquisition
    - The Evolving Landscape of Recruitment
    - The Promises and Pitfalls of AI-Powered Hiring
    - Defining Your Robo-Recruiting Strategy
- Leveraging AI for Candidate Sourcing
    - Automated Job Posting and Distribution
    - Intelligent Candidate Screening and Filtering
    - Predictive Analytics for Talent Identification
- Enhancing the Candidate Experience
    - Chatbots and Virtual Assistants
    - Gamification and Immersive Assessments
    - Personalized Candidate Engagement
- Streamlining the Hiring Process
    - Automated Interview Scheduling
    - AI-Powered Resume and Application Review
    - Intelligent Candidate Tracking and Workflow
- Optimizing Employee Onboarding
    - Automated Onboarding Checklists
    - AI-Driven Role Matching and Mentorship
    - Personalized Learning and Development
- Workforce Planning and Analytics
    - Predictive Hiring Demand Forecasting
    - AI-Powered Talent Gap Analysis
    - Data-Driven Succession Planning
- Intelligent Performance Management
    - Automated Goal Setting and Tracking
    - AI-Powered Performance Feedback and Reviews

- Personalized Learning Recommendations

- AI-Powered Employee Retention
  - Predictive Attrition Models
  - Personalized Retention Strategies
  - AI-Driven Employee Engagement

- Ethical Considerations in Robo-Recruiting
  - Addressing Bias and Fairness in AI
  - Ensuring Transparency and Accountability
  - Maintaining Human Oversight and Intervention

- Building an AI-Powered HR Consultancy
  - Developing Robo-Recruiting Service Offerings
  - Implementing AI-Driven Consulting Frameworks
  - Delivering Measurable Business Impact

- Aligning Technology and Human Expertise
  - Fostering Collaboration Between HR and IT
  - Upskilling HR Professionals in AI Literacy
  - Change Management and Organizational Readiness

- Navigating Regulatory Compliance
  - Adhering to Data Privacy and Security Standards
  - Ensuring Compliance with Labor and Employment Laws
  - Adapting to Evolving Regulations in Robo-Recruiting

- Marketing and Branding Your Robo-Recruiting Services
  - Crafting a Compelling Value Proposition
  - Developing Thought Leadership Content
  - Implementing Effective Sales and Marketing Strategies

- Building a Scalable Robo-Recruiting Platform
  - Selecting and Integrating AI Technologies
  - Ensuring Reliable and Secure Infrastructure
  - Maintaining Agility and Continuous Improvement

- The Future of Robo-Recruiting
  - Emerging Trends and Innovations in AI for HR

- Preparing for the Workforce of Tomorrow
- Envisioning the Next Generation of Talent Acquisition

The Rise of AI in Talent Acquisition

The Evolving Terrain of Recruitment

Gone are the days when recruitment was a simple matter of posting job ads and sifting through resumes. The world of talent acquisition has undergone a seismic shift, and it's all thanks to the rise of artificial intelligence (AI). Recruiters and HR professionals are embracing this radical technology, leveraging its power to optimize processes, improve candidate experience, and uncover top talent with unprecedented precision.

The traditional recruitment model, with its reliance on manual screening and subjective decision making, is rapidly becoming obsolete. AI powered tools have introduced a new era of data driven hiring, where algorithms can sift through vast candidate pools, identify the most promising individuals, and even predict job performance with uncanny accuracy. From automated job postings and intelligent candidate filtering to predictive analytics and personalized engagement, AI is redefining every aspect of the talent acquisition situation.

But this evolution isn't without its challenges. As AI becomes increasingly embedded in the hiring process, concerns around bias, fairness, and transparency have come to the forefront. Navigating these pitfalls requires a delicate balance, one that uses the power of AI while ensuring that human oversight and ethical considerations remain at the heart of talent acquisition strategies.

The Promises and Pitfalls of AI Powered Hiring

The allure of AI powered hiring is undeniable. With its ability to automate time consuming tasks, analyze vast troves of data, and make unbiased decisions, it promises to overhaul the way organizations identify, attract, and onboard top talent. From streamlining the candidate experience to optimizing the entire hiring funnel, the potential benefits of AI are vast and far reaching.

However, the implementation of AI in hiring is not without its risks. Algorithmic bias, a lack of transparency in decision making, and the potential for AI to perpetuate or even exacerbate existing societal inequalities are just a few of the challenges that organizations must grapple with. Failing to address these pitfalls can lead to disastrous consequences, from legal liabilities to damaged brand reputation and a loss of public trust.

Navigating the promises and pitfalls of AI powered hiring requires a comprehensive understanding of the technology's capabilities and limitations. It's critical for organizations to approach this transformation with a critical eye, prioritizing ethical considerations, ensuring human oversight, and promoting a culture of transparency and accountability. Only then can the true potential of AI be uncovered, authorizing talent acquisition teams to make data driven decisions and deliver exceptional hiring outcomes.

Defining Your Robo Recruiting Strategy

Embracing the power of AI in talent acquisition is no longer a luxury, but a necessity. As the competition for top talent intensifies, organizations that fail to employ this revolutionary technology risk falling behind. But crafting a successful "robo recruiting" strategy is no easy feat. It requires a deep understanding of the available AI powered solutions, a clear vision for how they can be integrated into the hiring process, and a steadfast commitment to ethical and responsible implementation.

The first step in defining your robo recruiting strategy is to conduct a thorough assessment of your current hiring practices. Identify the is a challenge, bottlenecks, and areas where AI can have the greatest impact. From there, you can begin to map out a comprehensive plan that harmonizes with your organization's broader talent management objectives and HR priorities.

Building a successful robo recruiting strategy also necessitates a collaborative approach, one that brings together HR professionals, IT experts, and business leaders. By nurturing cross functional alignment and ensuring that all stakeholders are on board, you can navigate the challenges and complexities of implementing AI powered hiring solutions with greater ease and confidence.

Ultimately, defining your robo recruiting strategy is not a one time exercise, but an ongoing process of refinement and adaptation. As the technology and regulatory situation evolve, your strategy must remain adaptable, responsive, and attuned to the changing needs of your organization and the broader talent market. By embracing this mindset of continuous improvement, you can position your organization at the forefront of the AI driven recruitment revolution.

Leveraging AI for Candidate Sourcing

Automated Job Posting and Distribution

In the cutthroat world of talent acquisition, efficiency is the name of the game. Why waste precious time and resources manually posting job ads across a dozen different platforms when AI can do it for you? Say goodbye to the days of copy pasting job descriptions and praying they land in the right inboxes. With automated job posting and distribution, your open positions will reach the far corners of the digital universe, scouring the innermost crevices of the internet to uncover the perfect candidates.

But this is no mere job board blitz - oh no, we're talking about a finely tuned, data driven machine. Our AI wizards have employed the power of machine learning to analyze job market trends, identify the best performing channels, and dynamically adjust your postings accordingly. It's like having a crystal ball that tells you exactly where to cast your net to reel in the big fish.

And the best part? Our system learns as it goes, constantly refining its approach to ensure your jobs are hitting the sweet spot. No more guesswork, no more crossing your fingers and hoping for the best. Just sit back, relax, and let the AI do the heavy lifting while you sip your lukewarm coffee and bask in the glory of your newfound hiring superpowers.

Intelligent Candidate Screening and Filtering

Ah, the dreaded resume avalanche - a mountain of qualifications, certifications, and buzzwords that would make even the most seasoned HR professional weep. But fear not, my friends, for AI is here to slay the paper dragon and bring order to the chaos.

Our intelligent candidate screening and filtering algorithms are like a highly caffeinated, precision guided magic wand. With the power of natural language processing and predictive analytics, we can scour through endless piles of applications, identifying the true gems that sync with your specific job requirements. No more tedious manual reviews, no more missing out on that perfect candidate hidden in the haystack.

But this is no mere keyword matching parlor trick. Our AI driven screening process goes far beyond surface level qualifications, delving into the deeper nuances of each applicant's experience, skills, and cultural fit. It's like having a team of expert headhunters on your payroll, with the added bonus of lightning fast processing and zero coffee breaks.

And the best part? Our system is constantly learning and adapting, refining its algorithms to become more accurate and insightful with each passing day. So you can rest assured that your candidate pool is always top notch, carefully curated to perfection by the tireless, ever vigilant AI overlords.

Predictive Analytics for Talent Identification

In the high stakes game of talent acquisition, being able to predict the future is the ultimate superpower. Imagine a world where you can pinpoint the exact moment a top tier candidate is about to hit the job market, or identify the hidden gems lurking in your own backyard, just waiting to be plucked from obscurity.

Well, buckle up, my friends, because that's exactly what our AI powered predictive analytics can do. By leveraging a vast trove of data, from job market trends to employment history patterns, our models can uncover understanding that would make even Nostradamus nod in approval.

Imagine being able to spot the next generation of rockstar software engineers before they even graduate, or knowing exactly when that skilled accountant in a neighboring company is about to get restless and start exploring new opportunities. It's like having your own crystal ball, only with a lot less mysticism and a lot more cold, hard data.

But don't worry, we're not just handing you a fancy dashboard and leaving you to your own devices. Our team of expert data scientists and AI gurus will work hand in-hand with you to develop a customized predictive model tailored to your unique hiring needs. Because at the end of the day, the true power of this technology lies in its ability to transform your talent acquisition strategy from reactive to proactive – and that's the kind of competitive edge that can make or break a business.

Improving the Candidate Experience

Chatbots and Virtual Assistants

In the fast paced world of modern recruitment, it's essential to rationalize the candidate experience and make it as fluid as possible. Enter the dynamic duo of chatbots and virtual assistants - your robot recruitment sidekicks that are ready to take the hiring process to new heights. Imagine a world where candidates can get instant answers to their burning questions, 24/7, without ever having to endure the dreaded hold music or endless email chains.

These AI powered conversational agents are like digital concierges, guiding candidates through every step of the application journey. From scheduling interviews to answering FAQs, they're the Swiss Army knives of the recruitment world. Imagine the delight on a candidate's face when they realize they can get their concerns addressed in a matter of seconds, without ever having to wait in line or play phone tag with a harried HR representative.

But these chatbots and virtual assistants are more than just glorified customer service bots - they're data driven, personalized experiences that can tailor the interaction to each individual's needs. By analyzing a candidate's interactions and preferences, these AI agents can provide hyper relevant information, offer customized suggestions, and even detect when a candidate might be feeling frustrated or discouraged, allowing them to offer a timely and empathetic response.

The best part? These AI assistants never get tired, never take a sick day, and never forget a detail. They're the ultimate recruitment sidekicks, working tirelessly to ensure that every candidate feels valued, supported, and engaged throughout the hiring process. So say goodbye to those awkward silences and clunky handoffs, and hello to a new era of fluid, delightful candidate experiences powered by the dynamic duo of chatbots and virtual assistants.

Gamification and Immersive Assessments

In the ever evolving world of talent acquisition, the days of the traditional, dry job application process are quickly becoming a relic of the past. Savvy recruiters are embracing the power of gamification and immersive assessments to transform the candidate experience into a truly engaging and memorable journey.

Imagine a scenario where, instead of mindlessly slogging through a stack of resumes, candidates are invited to participate in a high energy, interactive game that challenges their skills, problem solving abilities, and creative thinking. By gamifying the assessment process, employers can not only uncover a wealth of understanding about a candidate's true potential, but also capture the attention and enthusiasm of the next generation of top talent.

These immersive assessments go beyond the typical multiple choice tests or bland personality quizzes. They're dynamic, visually captivating experiences that might task candidates with navigating a virtual obstacle course, coding a real time strategy game, or even solving a crime scene investigation. The possibilities are as limitless as the human imagination – and the payoff can be game changing.

Not only do these gamified assessments provide a far more engaging and memorable experience for candidates, but they also deliver a wealth of valuable data for recruiters. By tracking metrics like problem solving skills, collaboration, and creative thinking, employers can gain a deeper understanding of a candidate's true capabilities and potential fit for the role.

So why settle for the same old, stale recruitment tactics when you can employ the power of gamification and immersive assessments to create a truly unforgettable candidate experience? It's time to bring the fun back into hiring and let the games begin!

Personalized Candidate Engagement

In the high stakes world of talent acquisition, the key to standing out from the competition is all about delivering a personalized, tailored experience for each and every candidate. Gone are the days of one size-fits all job postings and generic email templates – the modern day recruiter is a master of personalization, crafting engagement strategies that make candidates feel truly valued and understood.

Imagine a scenario where a prospective employee applies for a position and is immediately greeted by a personalized video message from the hiring manager, highlighting the unique attributes that make them a perfect fit for the role.

Or picture a candidate who receives a curated playlist of industry relevant podcasts and thought leadership articles, handpicked by the recruitment team to showcase their deep understanding of the candidate's interests and aspirations.

These personalized touches go beyond the surface level niceties – they're data driven, AI powered understanding that dive deep into the psyche of each individual candidate. By leveraging predictive analytics, machine learning, and a keen understanding of human behavior, recruiters can craft engagement strategies that appeal on a fundamental level, leaving candidates feeling truly seen, heard, and valued.

But the benefits of personalized candidate engagement extend far beyond the initial application process. Imagine a scenario where an AI powered virtual assistant regularly checks in with candidates, providing updates on the status of their application, offering encouragement and support, and even anticipating their needs before they arise. This level of proactive, personalized outreach can be the difference between a candidate feeling like a cog in the machine and a valued member of the team.

In a world where top talent is in high demand, the organizations that prioritize personalized candidate engagement will undoubtedly come out on top. So why settle for a one size-fits all approach when you can create a hiring experience that feels like it was custom tailored just for them? It's time to embrace the power of personalization and uncover the true potential of your recruitment efforts.

Streamlining the Hiring Process

Automated Interview Scheduling

In the fast paced world of modern recruitment, the traditional dance of back and-forth emails and phone tag to schedule interviews is as outdated as a floppy disk. Enter the revolutionary world of automated interview scheduling – a game changer that will have your HR team doing a happy robot dance (without the need for oil cans, of course).

Imagine a world where candidates can simply click a link, view available interview slots, and book their preferred time with a few taps of their finger. No more endless email chains, no more hunting down the hiring manager's calendar like a virtual private eye. Our AI powered scheduling assistants handle it all, syncing seamlessly with everyone's calendars to ensure smooth, conflict free scheduling.

But the benefits don't stop there. These scheduling bots can also send automated reminders, collect relevant information from candidates, and even reschedule appointments with the agility of a Cirque du Soleil performer. Goodbye, no shows and last minute cancellations – our robo recruiters have got your back.

And let's not forget the data goldmine. With every interview slot booked, our AI tracks patterns, identifies trends, and spits out perceptions that would make even the savviest HR guru salivate. Perfect your interview process, reduce hiring time, and watch your talent pipeline flow like a finely tuned robotic assembly line.

AI Powered Resume and Application Review

Ah, the dreaded resume review – the bane of every recruiter's existence. Wading through piles of CVs, deciphering cryptic job titles, and trying to distinguish genuine talent from creative fluff. It's enough to make even the most seasoned HR professional yearn for a career as a professional basket weaver.

Enter the AI cavalry, ready to charge into the resume review battlefield and emerge victorious. Our cutting edge algorithms can sift through thousands of applications in mere seconds, identifying the true gems with the precision of a diamond cutter. No more squinting at blurry PDFs or trying to decode emojis in cover letters – our robo recruiters have got this covered.

But it's not just about speed; it's about smarts. Our AI powered systems can dig deeper, uncovering hidden talents, spotting potential red flags, and providing real time feedback to hiring managers. Imagine the power of having an army of virtual assistants, each with the analytical prowess of a data scientist and the intuition of a seasoned HR pro.

And the best part? Our AI driven application review process is designed to be fair, unbiased, and transparent. No more worrying about unconscious biases creeping into the hiring equation – our robo recruiters are laser focused on finding the best candidates, regardless of their background or personal attributes.

Intelligent Candidate Tracking and Workflow

Keeping track of candidates as they navigate the hiring pipeline can be a herculean task, akin to trying to herd a pack of hyperactive kittens. But fear not, for our AI powered candidate tracking and workflow solutions are here to bring order to the chaos.

Imagine a centralized hub where every candidate interaction, document, and decision is meticulously tracked and organized. Our intelligent systems can monitor the progress of each applicant, flag potential bottlenecks, and even suggest the next best steps to keep the hiring process humming along like a well oiled machine.

But it's not just about managing the logistics – our AI driven workflows can also help you make smarter, more informed decisions. By analyzing vast troves of data, our systems can identify patterns, predict outcomes, and offer real time recommendations to perfect your hiring process.

Goodbye, disjointed spreadsheets and forgotten follow ups. Hello, continuous collaboration, improved transparency, and the ability to make data driven decisions that will have your hiring managers high fiving like they just won the Super Bowl (without the risk of accidentally breaking any robotic limbs, of course).

Optimizing Employee Onboarding

Automated Onboarding Checklists

The days of haphazard employee onboarding are long gone. In the age of Robo Recruiting, the onboarding process has undergone a remarkable transformation, thanks to the power of automation. Gone are the piles of paperwork and the convoluted checklists that used to haunt new hires. Instead, we've ushered in a new era of smooth, AI driven onboarding that makes efficient the entire experience.

Imagine a world where the moment a new employee accepts an offer, an elaborate onboarding sequence is set in motion. From the completion of essential paperwork to the scheduling of vital training sessions, every step is meticulously orchestrated by a virtual assistant that never forgets a thing. No more scrambling to ensure all the i's are dotted and t's are crossed - the AI takes care of it all, freeing up your HR team to focus on the more personalized aspects of onboarding.

But the benefits of automated checklists go far beyond mere efficiency. By leveraging machine learning algorithms, the system can adapt to the unique needs and preferences of each new hire, ensuring that the onboarding experience is tailored to their specific requirements. Whether it's streamlining the setup of company accounts or ensuring that critical compliance training is completed on time, the AI powered onboarding checklists are the unsung heroes of the modern workplace.

AI Driven Role Matching and Mentorship

Onboarding is not just about the administrative tasks - it's about setting new hires up for long term success. And that's where the true power of AI driven role matching and mentorship comes into play. By analyzing a wealth of data points, from skills and experience to personality traits and cultural fit, the Robo Recruiting system can identify the ideal mentors and peer to-peer connections for each new employee.

Imagine a world where a new software engineer doesn't just get a generic welcome package, but is seamlessly paired with a seasoned developer who shares their passion for cutting edge technologies and unceasing problem solving. Or a marketing associate who is automatically matched with a mentor who has a proven track record of creating viral content and building engaging brand narratives. The AI doesn't just place warm bodies in seats - it orchestrates strategic pairings that encourage genuine, meaningful connections and accelerate the new hire's integration into the team.

But the magic doesn't stop there. The AI powered mentorship program also taps into the collective wisdom of the organization, identifying the best suited subject matter experts to provide targeted guidance and support. Want to learn the ins and outs of the company's proprietary CRM system? The AI will connect you with the superstar who wrote the book on it. Eager to level up your presentation skills? The AI will find the charismatic executive who can share their secrets for captivating an audience.

Personalized Learning and Development

In the world of Robo Recruiting, onboarding is not just about the first few weeks - it's an ongoing journey of growth and development. And thanks to the power of AI, the learning and development opportunities for new hires have never been more personalized and effective.

Imagine a scenario where a newly minted sales associate is onboarded with a tailored curriculum that combines online training modules, interactive simulations, and hands on coaching sessions. The AI system doesn't just assign generic courses - it analyzes the individual's strengths, weaknesses, and learning preferences to craft a custom learning plan that accelerates their mastery of the role.

But the real magic happens when the AI driven learning program seamlessly adapts to the new hire's progress. As they complete modules and demonstrate proficiency, the system automatically makes accessible new challenges and opportunities for growth. It's like having a personal trainer for your career, constantly pushing you to reach new heights and providing the support you need to succeed.

And let's not forget the power of AI powered performance monitoring and feedback. By continuously tracking the new hire's progress and performance, the system can provide real time understanding and personalized recommendations for improvement. Struggling with a particular sales technique? The AI will identify the areas for growth and suggest targeted training sessions. Excelling in client interactions? The system will flag the employee for potential leadership opportunities.

In the end, the AI powered onboarding experience is not just about efficiency and compliance - it's about revealing the true potential of every new hire. By seamlessly blending automation, personalization, and continuous learning, the Robo Recruiting approach to onboarding sets the stage for a workforce that is engaged, equipped, and poised for long term success.

Workforce Planning and Analytics

Predictive Hiring Demand Forecasting

In the ever evolving situation of the talent market, the ability to predict hiring demands with pinpoint accuracy can give your Robo Recruiting consultancy a decisive edge. Forget the days of gazing into a crystal ball and hoping for the best - with the power of AI driven predictive analytics, you'll be able to forecast hiring needs with the precision of a master chess player. Imagine the look on your clients' faces when you confidently declare that they'll need to hire 27.8 data scientists and 12.4 user experience designers six months from now. It's the kind of sorcery that will have them begging you to share your secrets.

The key is to feed your algorithms a steady diet of data - everything from industry trends and economic forecasts to your clients' historical hiring patterns and growth projections. By crunching these numbers with the constant efficiency of a supercomputer, your Robo Recruiting platform will be able to sniff out hiring needs before they even materialize. And the best part? Your clients will think you have a crystal ball, when in reality, you've channeled the power of machine learning to become a talent acquisition oracle.

Of course, fine tuning your predictive models will require a delicate dance between data science and... well, actual science. You'll need to experiment, tweak, and refine your algorithms until they're as accurate as a Swiss watch. But trust me, the payoff will be worth it. Imagine being able to have a client's entire hiring roadmap mapped out before they even utter the words "We need to grow our team." That's the kind of competitive advantage that will have your competitors green with envy.

AI Powered Talent Gap Analysis

In the high stakes world of talent acquisition, identifying and bridging skill gaps is the key to uncovering your clients' full potential. And with the help of AI, you'll be able to conduct talent gap analyses with the precision of a surgeon and the foresight of a Jedi master.

Imagine a world where you can effortlessly sift through mountains of data - everything from employee profiles and performance reviews to market trends and industry benchmarks - and pinpoint the exact skills your clients' teams are missing. It's like having a crystal ball that can see into the future and tell you exactly what kind of talent your clients will need to stay ahead of the curve.

But the real magic happens when you start connecting the dots. By leveraging predictive analytics and machine learning, your Robo Recruiting platform will be able to identify emerging skill gaps before they even materialize. It's like having a talent acquisition sixth sense - you'll be able to spot the gaps and then swoop in with a customized plan to fill them before your clients even realize they have a problem.

And the best part? You'll be able to present your findings in a way that will have your clients marveling at your incredible foresight. Forget those boring PowerPoint slides - with the power of AI, you'll be able to create interactive dashboards and data visualizations that will have your clients nodding along, wide eyed and utterly convinced of your talent acquisition prowess.

Data Driven Succession Planning

In the high stakes world of talent acquisition, succession planning is the ultimate chess game. And with the help of AI, you'll be able to take your clients' succession strategies to the next level. Forget about relying on gut instincts and personal biases - your Robo Recruiting platform will be able to analyze mountains of data and identify the perfect candidates to fill key roles, before your clients even realize they have a gap to fill.

Imagine being able to pinpoint the precise skills and competencies needed for a critical leadership position, and then using AI powered predictive analytics to scour your client's talent pool and uncover the hidden gems that are primed for promotion. It's like having a crystal ball that can see into the future and tell you exactly who's going to be the next CEO or CTO.

But the real magic happens when you start to weave in personalized development plans. By tapping into the power of AI, you'll be able to create customized training and mentorship programs that will help your clients' high potential employees bridge any skill gaps and prepare for their next big role. Imagine the look on your clients' faces when you present them with a detailed succession plan that not only identifies the perfect candidates, but also lays out a step by-step roadmap for helping them reach the next level.

And the best part? You'll be able to do all of this with the efficiency and precision of a well oiled machine. No more relying on outdated spreadsheets or gut instincts - your Robo Recruiting platform will be able to crunch the numbers, analyze the data, and deliver a succession plan that will have your clients begging for more.

Intelligent Performance Management

Automated Goal Setting and Tracking

Gone are the days when performance management was a rigid, top down exercise. With the power of AI, we can finally bid farewell to those cumbersome yearly reviews and say hello to a whole new era of intelligent, personalized goal setting and tracking. Imagine a world where your employees' professional aspirations are seamlessly harmonized with your organization's strategic objectives - without the endless back-and-forth and dreaded spreadsheet marathons.

Our AI powered performance management system does the heavy lifting for you, analyzing each employee's unique skills, interests, and career trajectory to recommend tailored goals that inspire and challenge them. But we don't stop there. Using predictive analytics, the system continuously monitors progress and identifies potential roadblocks, proactively suggesting adjustments to keep your team on track and motivated.

No more passive aggressive Slack messages about overdue quarterly check ins. Our platform automates the entire goal setting and tracking process, sending timely reminders, facilitating peer feedback, and generating real time performance dashboards that give both managers and employees a clear line of sight into their progress. It's a win win for everyone - your employees feel allowed and engaged, while you enjoy the peace of mind that comes with a highly effective, data driven performance management strategy.

AI Powered Performance Feedback and Reviews

Forget the days of awkward, anxiety inducing performance reviews. Our AI powered feedback and review system brings a whole new level of sophistication and personalization to the table. By analyzing a wealth of data points - from communication patterns and collaboration trends to sentiment analysis and 360 degree feedback - our platform delivers tailored, objective understanding that help your employees understand their strengths, identify areas for growth, and uncover their full potential.

But we're not just about pointing out the gaps; our AI also provides useful recommendations for professional development, whether it's suggesting relevant training programs, recommending mentorship opportunities, or identifying potential lateral moves that could be a game changer for their career. And the best part? This intelligent feedback loop is a continuous process, not a once a-year chore, ensuring your team is always progressing and evolving.

Imagine the relief your managers will feel when they no longer have to dread those dreaded review meetings, armed with little more than subjective observations and gut feelings. Our AI augmented approach takes the guesswork out of performance management, providing data driven perceptions that nurture honest, productive conversations and set the stage for genuine growth and development. It's a true game changer for organizations looking to create a culture of continuous improvement and empowerment.

Personalized Learning Recommendations

In the fast paced, constantly evolving world of business, the ability to upskill and reskill your workforce is the key to staying ahead of the curve. But let's be honest, traditional one size-fits all training programs are about as exciting as watching paint dry. That's where our AI powered learning recommendations come in to save the day.

By analyzing each employee's unique skills, interests, and career aspirations, our platform identifies personalized learning opportunities that match with their professional goals and ignite their passion. Forget the generic online courses and boring lunch and-learn sessions - our system taps into a vast system of cutting edge content, from immersive VR simulations to interactive microlearning modules, to deliver a truly tailored learning experience.

But it's not just about the content; our AI also monitors engagement and performance, adjusting the recommendations in real time to ensure your employees are constantly challenged and motivated. Imagine the boost in morale and retention when your team feels like their professional development is a top priority, not an afterthought. With our intelligent learning platform, you'll make accessible a highly skilled, future ready workforce that's poised to take your organization to new heights.

AI Powered Employee Retention

Predictive Attrition Models

Employee retention is a tricky beast, but fear not, my friends - with the power of AI on our side, we can tame that wild stallion and keep our top talent happily galloping along. It all starts with predictive attrition models, a fancy term for using data and machine learning to forecast which of our employees might be eyeing the exit door.

Forget the old school methods of relying on gut feelings and exit interviews - that's so last century. Now, we can crunch the numbers, analyze the trends, and spot the warning signs long before they become a full blown resignation. Think of it as a crystal ball for your workforce, except instead of gazing into a mystic orb, we're crunching petabytes of data and training neural networks.

By tapping into a wealth of information - from performance reviews and job satisfaction surveys to social media activity and even the frequency of bathroom breaks - our AI models can identify the key indicators that an employee might be ready to fly the coop. And the best part? These models don't just spit out generic predictions, but they can get specific, pinpointing the precise reasons why someone might be considering a career change.

Armed with this intel, HR teams can spring into action, crafting personalized retention strategies tailored to each individual's needs and concerns. So, instead of waiting for the resignation letter to arrive, we can get proactive, nipping the problem in the bud before it even becomes an issue. It's like having a crystal ball, a fortune teller, and a personal life coach all rolled into one AI powered package.

Personalized Retention Strategies

Alright, so we've got the data, we've got the predictive models - now, it's time to put that intel to work and keep our top talent right where they belong. And let me tell you, gone are the days of one size-fits all employee retention strategies. In the age of Robo Recruiting, it's all about getting personal.

Picture this: your AI system has flagged that your star salesperson, Maria, is at risk of leaving. But it's not because she's unhappy with her paycheck or her benefits package - no, the data shows that she's feeling underappreciated and craving more opportunities for growth and development.

Armed with this insight, you can swiftly spring into action, crafting a personalized retention strategy that speaks directly to Maria's needs. Maybe that means setting up a mentorship program where she can learn from the top performing sales reps, or offering her the chance to spearhead a new client facing initiative. The key is to address the specific factors that are driving her restlessness, not just throw generic perks and bonuses her way.

And it's not just about the big gestures, either. Sometimes, it's the little things that can make all the difference – things like prioritizing one on-one check ins, ensuring her workload is manageable, or even surprising her with tickets to that niche indie concert she's been dying to attend. The more personalized and thoughtful we can be, the more likely we are to keep our top talent firmly in the fold.

So, forget the days of the generic "employee of the month" award or the dreaded "team building" exercises. In the world of Robo Recruiting, it's all about crafting retention strategies that are as unique and tailored as the individuals we're trying to keep happy and engaged.

AI Driven Employee Engagement

Alright, let's talk about employee engagement – that elusive unicorn that every HR professional is chasing. In the past, we've relied on tedious surveys, clunky suggestion boxes, and the occasional pizza party to try and gauge how engaged our workforce is. But in the age of Robo Recruiting, we've got a secret weapon: AI driven employee engagement.

Imagine a world where your AI system is constantly monitoring the pulse of your organization, picking up on subtle shifts in mood, productivity, and morale. It's like having a virtual finger on the collective heartbeat of your team, and it allows us to address issues before they balloon into full blown crises.

Think about it – your AI can analyze everything from Slack conversations and email patterns to performance metrics and social media activity, identifying the early warning signs of disengagement. Maybe it notices that one of your developers has been logging fewer hours or that a usually vocal team member has gone mysteriously quiet in the company wide chat. Armed with this intel, you can swoop in, find out what's going on, and take proactive steps to re engage that individual before they start polishing up their résumé.

But it's not just about identifying problems – our AI driven engagement tools can also help us celebrate victories and encourage a genuine sense of community. Imagine a system that automatically generates personalized congratulatory messages when an employee hits a milestone or that surfaces heartfelt peer to-peer shoutouts in real time. It's like having a virtual cheerleader squad, always there to pump up the team and keep morale sky high.

And the best part? Our AI can continuously learn and evolve, adapting its engagement strategies to the unique needs and preferences of each employee. So, while the old school methods of employee engagement might have felt like a one size-fits all approach, our Robo Recruiting solutions can tailor the experience to the individual, creating a truly personalized and rewarding experience for every member of the team.

Ethical Considerations in Robo Recruiting

Addressing Bias and Fairness in AI

Let's be real, folks - when it comes to AI, bias is like that pesky cousin who just won't stop crashing your pool party. It's always lurking, waiting to ruin the fun. But fear not, my friends, for we shall confront this challenge head on. Because let's face it, if we're going to build a robo recruiting empire, we need to make sure it's as unbiased as a robot's poker face.

First and foremost, we need to get up close and personal with our AI systems. Understand their inner workings, their training data, and their decision making processes. It's like performing an AI colonoscopy - yeah, it might be a little uncomfortable, but it's the only way to spot those hidden biases lurking in the shadows.

Next, we need to implement rigorous testing protocols. Throw every curve ball we can at our AI models - resume names that scream "diversity," job descriptions that sound like they were written by a robot on a sugar high, the whole shebang. If our robo recruiter can't handle the heat, it's time to go back to the drawing board and whip it into shape.

And let's not forget about the human element. Because no matter how smart our AI might be, it's still going to need a little guidance from the meatbags. That's where diversity and inclusivity in our hiring teams come into play. Diversity isn't just a buzzword, folks - it's the key to making accessible a more balanced and fair recruitment process.

Ensuring Transparency and Accountability

Ah, transparency and accountability - the dynamic duo of ethical robo recruiting. It's like trying to host a magic show without any sleight of hand. Sure, it might be a little more work, but trust me, your audience (aka, the candidates) will appreciate the honesty.

First up, we need to be crystal clear about how our AI systems work. No more of this "it's a black box" nonsense. We're talking open kimono, people. Lay out the algorithms, the data sources, the decision making criteria - the whole shebang. Because let's be real, if we can't explain it to a room full of five year-olds, it's probably not going to fly with the legal team.

And when it comes to accountability, we need to embrace it like a long lost friend. Establish clear guidelines and protocols for monitoring the performance of our AI systems, and be prepared to own up to any hiccups or misfires. After all, the last thing we want is for our robo recruiting empire to come crashing down because of a rogue algorithm gone wild.

But it's not just about accountability for the technology - we need to extend that same level of transparency and accountability to our human decision makers as well. Because let's face it, even the smartest AI is still going to need a little human oversight and intervention. And we need to make sure those humans are playing by the rules, too.

Maintaining Human Oversight and Intervention

Alright, let's talk about the elephant in the room - the fact that no matter how sophisticated our robo recruiting systems might be, they're still going to need a little human touch. And that's not a bad thing, my friends. In fact, it's downright essential.

Think about it this way - our AI models are like the world's most impressive juggling act. They can handle a dozen balls at once, no problem. But what happens when a new, unexpected ball gets thrown into the mix? That's where our human experts come in, ready to swoop in and keep the show going.

We need to build in strong systems for human oversight and intervention, where our recruitment professionals can step in and make those critical, precise decisions that even the smartest AI might struggle with. Maybe it's a candidate with an unconventional background who might not tick all the boxes, but could be a perfect fit. Or maybe it's a role that requires a level of emotional intelligence that our robo recruiter just can't replicate.

And let's not forget about the importance of maintaining human accountability. Because at the end of the day, even the most advanced AI system is still a tool, and it's up to us, the humans, to wield it responsibly and ethically. We need to ensure that our decision makers are well trained, enabled, and held to the highest standards of transparency and accountability.

Building an AI Powered HR Consultancy

Developing Robo Recruiting Service Options

As the world of talent acquisition evolves, the time has come to embrace the power of AI and craft a suite of Robo Recruiting services that will leave your clients in awe. Forget the one size-fits all approach – it's time to get creative, folks. Think outside the box and leave those stuffy HR templates in the dust.

Start by conducting a detailed examination into your client's unique needs and is a difficulty. Do they struggle with sifting through mountains of resumes? Are they constantly playing phone tag to schedule interviews? Or maybe they're drowning in onboarding paperwork. Whatever their Achilles' heel, you're going to fix it with a dose of cutting edge AI magic.

Now, let's talk about building your service menu. Automated candidate sourcing? Check. Intelligent resume screening? You bet. Personalized onboarding experiences? Ding, ding, ding – we have a winner! But don't stop there. Get wild and crazy with virtual job fairs, gamified assessments, and AI powered career coaches. The key is to stay ahead of the curve and offer solutions your clients didn't even know they needed.

And let's not forget about the all important human touch. Sure, AI is the star of the show, but your consultants need to be the stage managers who ensure the performance is flawless. Develop training programs that enable your team to seamlessly blend technology and 人 expertise, creating a symphony of talent acquisition magic.

Implementing AI Driven Consulting Frameworks

Now that you've got your Robo Recruiting services locked and loaded, it's time to put the pedal to the metal and create a world class consulting framework. No more generic PowerPoint presentations and one size-fits all recommendations. Your clients deserve a tailor made experience that leaves them wondering, "How did they know what I was thinking?"

Start by building a comprehensive assessment process that investigates deep into your client's unique hiring challenges. Apply AI powered diagnostic tools to uncover hidden patterns, identify talent gaps, and pinpoint areas for improvement. But don't stop there – weave in a healthy dose of human intuition, because sometimes the best solutions come from the most unexpected places.

Next, it's time to develop your AI driven consulting methodology. Forget the traditional linear approach; instead, embrace a dynamic, cyclical framework that adapts to your client's evolving needs. Implement an adaptable mindset, where you're constantly gathering feedback, testing new ideas, and refining your strategies.

And let's not forget about the all important data and analytics component. Apply the power of predictive models, real time observations, and AI powered forecasting to provide your clients with a crystal ball into their future talent pipeline. But remember, data is only as good as the story you tell with it. Craft compelling narratives that inspire action and leave your clients saying, "Wow, I never thought of it that way!"

Delivering Measurable Business Impact

As an AI powered HR consultancy, your ultimate goal is to deliver tangible, measurable results that have a real impact on your clients' businesses. Gone are the days of fluffy metrics and vanity KPIs – it's time to show them the money, folks.

Start by harmonizing your service products and consulting frameworks with your clients' most pressing business objectives. Are they struggling with high turnover? Develop a personalized retention strategy powered by predictive attrition models and AI driven employee engagement initiatives. Trying to scale their workforce rapidly? Apply AI powered hiring demand forecasting and intelligent talent pipeline management to ensure they have the right people in the right roles at the right time.

But don't just stop at the "what" – make sure you're also capturing the "why" and the "how." Implement sturdy tracking and reporting mechanisms that showcase the true business impact of your Robo Recruiting solutions. Quantify the cost savings, productivity gains, and revenue increases that your clients are experiencing, and present the data in a way that's both visually stunning and easy to understand.

And let's not forget about the intangible benefits. Sure, the numbers are important, but your clients also want to feel the love. Develop a strong feedback loop that allows you to continuously gather understanding and testimonials, highlighting the ways your AI powered HR consultancy has transformed the lives of their employees and improved their overall organizational culture.

At the end of the day, your Robo Recruiting services are only as valuable as the real world impact they have on your clients' businesses. So, roll up your sleeves, get creative, and show them what the power of AI can do when it's wielded by a team of HR rockstars.

Matching Technology and Human Expertise

Promoting Collaboration Between HR and IT

In the ever evolving terrain of AI powered recruitment, the harmonious collaboration between HR and IT professionals is nothing short of very important. These two powerhouses, often viewed as polar opposites, must come together and forge an unbreakable alliance if your Robo Recruiting consultancy is to thrive.

Picture this: your HR team, brimming with expertise in talent management and people dynamics, possesses a deep understanding of the nuances that make a candidate tick. Meanwhile, your IT wizards, fluent in the language of ones and zeros, hold the keys to making accessible the full potential of AI and automation. When these two forces collide, magic happens.

It's time to ditch the silos and embrace a culture of collaboration. Encourage regular cross functional meetings, where the HR and IT teams can openly share their challenges, brainstorm solutions, and coordinate on a unified vision for your Robo Recruiting initiatives. Nurture an environment of mutual respect and a genuine appreciation for each other's strengths. After all, the true power lies in the teamwork of these two complementary skill sets.

Establish a dedicated "AI Taskforce" made up of HR and IT professionals, tasked with spearheading the adoption and implementation of AI driven tools and processes. This cross functional team will be instrumental in identifying the right technologies, ensuring uninterrupted integration, and supporting the change within your organization.

Remember, the road to AI powered recruitment is paved with both technological advancements and human expertise. By breaking down the barriers and cultivating a collaborative mindset, you'll uncover unprecedented levels of innovation, efficiency, and, most importantly, results for your clients.

Upskilling HR Professionals in AI Literacy

In the rapidly evolving world of Robo Recruiting, the ability to navigate the intricacies of AI driven technology is no longer a nice to-have - it's an absolute necessity. Your HR professionals, the supports of your client's talent strategies, must be equipped with a strong foundation in AI literacy to truly uncover the full potential of these life-changing tools.

Embrace a comprehensive training program that immerses your HR team in the world of AI, from the fundamentals of machine learning to the practical applications within the talent acquisition and management scene. Invite industry experts, data scientists, and software engineers to share their knowledge and understanding, nurturing a deeper understanding of the underlying algorithms, data processing, and decision making mechanisms that power these cutting edge solutions.

Go beyond the theoretical and dive into hands on workshops, where your HR professionals can explore the various AI powered tools and platforms at their fingertips. Encourage them to experiment, tinker, and get their hands dirty, allowing them to become confident and proficient users of these revolutionary technologies.

But the learning journey doesn't stop there. Establish a culture of continuous learning and development, where your HR team is constantly expanding their AI knowledge and skills. Invest in ongoing training programs, industry conferences, and peer to-peer knowledge sharing sessions to ensure your Robo Recruiting experts are always at the forefront of the latest advancements and recommended approaches.

Remember, an AI literate HR team is not only essential for the successful implementation of your Robo Recruiting services, but it also positions your consultancy as a trusted partner that truly understands the intersection of technology and human capital. Embrace this upskilling initiative and watch your HR professionals transform into AI powered talent wizards, ready to remake the way your clients find, hire, and manage their most valuable asset - their people.

Change Management and Organizational Readiness

Navigating the transition to an AI powered Robo Recruiting consultancy is a delicate and diverse endeavor, requiring a well crafted change management strategy to ensure uninterrupted implementation and organizational readiness. After all, the introduction of radical technologies can be met with resistance, skepticism, and a natural human aversion to the unknown.

Embrace a proactive approach to change management, starting with a comprehensive assessment of your client's organizational culture, mindsets, and existing processes. Identify the potential is a problem, areas of resistance, and key stakeholders who will play a central role in driving the adoption of your Robo Recruiting solutions.

Develop a comprehensive change management plan that addresses every step of the transition, from initial awareness and buy in to ongoing support and continuous improvement. Engage your client's leadership team, HR professionals, and end users in the process, ensuring they are active participants in shaping the future of their talent management strategies.

Craft a compelling narrative that highlights the tangible benefits of AI powered recruitment, from increased efficiency and data driven decision making to improved candidate experiences and improved hiring outcomes. Dispel the myths and misconceptions surrounding AI, emphasizing the role of human expertise in guiding and optimizing these radical tools.

Implement a sturdy training and communication plan that equips your client's stakeholders with the knowledge and skills necessary to embrace the Robo Recruiting transition. Offer hands on workshops, interactive demos, and ongoing support resources to nurture a sense of ownership and empowerment among your client's teams.

Most importantly, maintain a keen eye on organizational readiness, continuously monitoring the pulse of your client's workforce and adapting your change management strategies as needed. Be prepared to address emerging concerns, provide real time support, and celebrate the small victories along the way, solidifying your position as a trusted partner in their Robo Recruiting journey.

Remember, successful AI implementation is not just about the technology - it's about the people. By prioritizing change management and organizational readiness, you'll ensure a continuous and sustainable transformation, paving the way for your Robo Recruiting consultancy to thrive in the dynamic and ever evolving world of talent acquisition.

Navigating Regulatory Compliance

Adhering to Data Privacy and Security Standards

In the high stakes world of Robo Recruiting, data privacy and security are more than just buzzwords - they're the bedrock upon which your entire operation must be built. As you employ the power of AI to rationalize your hiring processes, you'll be entrusted with a goldmine of sensitive candidate information. And let me tell you, if that data falls into the wrong hands, it'll be a PR nightmare that makes your worst client pitch look like a walk in the park.

That's why it's essential to stay on top of the ever evolving terrain of data regulations. From the European Union's GDPR to the California Consumer Privacy Act, the rules of the game are changing faster than you can say "algorithmic bias." But don't let that scare you – think of it as a challenge to be conquered, a puzzle to be solved with all the ingenuity and creativity your Robo Recruiting wizards can muster.

Start by conducting a thorough audit of your data collection, storage, and usage practices. Identify any potential vulnerabilities and work with your legal and IT teams to shore them up. Implement strong encryption protocols, secure access controls, and iron clad data retention policies. And for goodness' sake, keep those software updates coming – hackers are always one step ahead, and you can't afford to be the low hanging fruit.

But it's not just about protecting your own systems - you'll also need to ensure that your AI powered tools and algorithms are up to snuff when it comes to data privacy. Carefully vet your vendors and partners, and don't be afraid to ask the tough questions. After all, your reputation is on the line, and one data breach could send your Robo Recruiting empire crumbling faster than a house of cards in a hurricane.

Ensuring Compliance with Labor and Employment Laws

If navigating the murky waters of data privacy and security wasn't enough, get ready to dive headfirst into the tangled web of labor and employment regulations. Because when you're using AI to simplify the hiring process, you're not just dealing with bits and bytes - you're dealing with human beings. And trust me, the lawmakers of the world have a lot to say about how you can (and can't) interact with those squishy, emotion filled creatures.

From anti discrimination laws to fair hiring practices, the compliance scene is a minefield that requires a deft touch and a keen understanding of the ever evolving legal situation. And let's not forget about those pesky union rules and collective bargaining agreements - you don't want to be the one who accidentally triggers a worker revolt with your shiny new AI powered recruiting tools.

The key is to stay vigilant and proactive. Regularly review your hiring processes and algorithms to ensure they're not inadvertently introducing bias or discriminating against protected classes. Collaborate closely with your legal team to ensure every step of your Robo Recruiting strategy is buttoned up and bulletproof. And keep a close eye on legislative developments - because you can bet that as AI becomes more omnipresent in the world of talent acquisition, the lawmakers will be hot on your heels, ready to pounce on any perceived misstep.

Remember, compliance isn't just about avoiding lawsuits and fines - it's about maintaining the trust and confidence of your clients and candidates. One wrong move, and you could find yourself a pariah in the Robo Recruiting community, blacklisted faster than a bot caught spamming LinkedIn."

Adapting to Evolving Regulations in Robo Recruiting

Let's be honest, the world of Robo Recruiting is a rapidly evolving situation, and the rules of the game are changing faster than an AI can crunch through a resume. Just when you think you've got a handle on all the regulatory hoops you need to jump through, along comes a new law, a fresh court ruling, or a scathing exposé that turns everything on its head.

But fear not, my Robo Recruiting warriors - this is where your nimbleness and adaptability will shine. Because in this game, the only constant is change, and the ability to adapt and adjust on the fly will be the key to your long term success.

Start by establishing a dedicated team of compliance experts, legal eagles, and AI ethicists who can stay on top of the latest developments in the field. Encourage them to network with industry peers, attend conferences, and scan the horizon for any signs of impending regulatory shifts. Because trust me, you don't want to be the one caught flat footed when the compliance police come knocking.

And when those changes do come – and they will, with the persistent regularity of a metronome on a caffeine bender – be ready to act swiftly and decisively. Revamp your processes, retrain your algorithms, and communicate transparently with your clients and candidates. After all, the last thing you want is for your shiny new Robo Recruiting tools to become the subject of a scathing viral exposé that makes you the laughingstock of the industry.

Remember, the world of Robo Recruiting is a ever evolving scene, and the only way to stay ahead of the curve is to be constantly on the lookout for the next big thing. So keep your ear to the ground, your finger on the pulse, and your AI powered recruiting tools in tip top shape. Because when the compliance cops come calling, you'll be ready to dance circles around them, one step ahead of the game."

Marketing and Branding Your Robo Recruiting Services

Crafting a Compelling Value Proposition

In the wild west of robo recruiting, standing out from the herd is no easy feat. But fear not, my friends, for I'm about to share the secrets to crafting a value proposition that'll have clients begging to hop on your AI powered bandwagon.

First things first, ditch the generic "we'll make your hiring process more efficient" spiel. That's about as exciting as watching paint dry. Instead, channel your inner unicorn and think big - I'm talking laser guided candidate missiles that can zero in on your perfect hire, faster than a cheetah chasing a cheeseburger.

But don't just take my word for it. Back that bad boy up with some hard hitting stats that'll make your clients' eyes light up like a Vegas casino. How about a 50% reduction in time to-hire? Or a 75% boost in employee retention? Sprinkle in a few case studies of your robo recruiting wizardry, and you've got a value proposition that'll have them signing on the dotted line faster than you can say "algorithmic sorcery."

And let's not forget the personal touch, because in this game, it's all about building relationships. Forget the cookie cutter, one size-fits all approach - tailor your value proposition to each client's unique needs, like a master couturier crafting a custom gown for a demanding diva. Show them you're not just another AI powered recruitment agency, but a strategic partner who understands their business inside and out.

Developing Thought Leadership Content

Now that you've got your value proposition locked and loaded, it's time to start flexing those thought leadership muscles. Because in the world of robo recruiting, the one with the biggest megaphone often wins the game.

Begin by positioning yourself as the resident oracle of all things AI and talent acquisition. Scribble down a content calendar that would make even the most seasoned marketing guru blush - we're talking blog posts, webinars, podcasts, and even the occasional interpretive dance number (hey, you never know what might go viral).

But don't just regurgitate the same old platitudes about the "future of work" and "the rise of the machines." Aim higher, my friends. Dive deep into the uncharted territories of robo recruiting, exploring the ethical quandaries, the technical nitty gritty, and the real world applications that'll have your audience captivated like a group of toddlers watching a magician pull a rabbit out of a hat.

And remember, when it comes to thought leadership, it's not just about quantity - it's about quality. Craft content that's so juicy, so irresistible, that your clients will be compelled to share it with their network faster than a wildfire spreading through a tinder dry forest. Think bold, think provocative, think "I can't believe they just said that!" Because in the world of robo recruiting, the ones who dare to be different are the ones who rise to the top.

Implementing Effective Sales and Marketing Strategies

Alright, now that you've got your value proposition and thought leadership content locked and loaded, it's time to put on your marketing superhero cape and free your inner Houdini.

First, let's talk about the sales side of the equation. Forget the old school, high pressure tactics - this is the age of the AI driven revolution, baby. Instead, focus on building genuine, human connections with your potential clients. Get to know them, understand their is a problem, and tailor your pitch to their unique needs. Because let's be real, no one wants to feel like they're just another number in your robotic sales funnel.

And when it comes to marketing, it's time to get creative. Ditch the boring, corporate brochures and embrace the wild, the wacky, and the downright unexpected. Think larger than-life billboards that'll have passersby doing double takes, or guerrilla marketing stunts that'll have the entire city buzzing about your robo recruiting prowess.

But don't forget the digital realm, either. Use the power of social media to showcase your thought leadership and connect with your target audience. And when it comes to lead generation, get ready to release your inner data scientist. Channel the power of predictive analytics, SEO, and targeted advertising to identify and engage with the perfect clients, like a cyber detective tracking down a high profile fugitive.

Ultimately, the key to effective sales and marketing in the world of robo recruiting is to embrace the unexpected, the unconventional, and the downright audacious. Because in this game, the ones who dare to be different are the ones who come out on top.

Building a Expandable Robo Recruiting Platform

Selecting and Integrating AI Technologies

When it comes to building a adaptable robo recruiting platform, the key is to select the right AI technologies and seamlessly integrate them into your HR processes. It's a delicate dance, my friends, where you need to balance cutting edge capabilities with good old fashioned reliability. Trust me, you don't want to be that agency that boasts about their "revolutionary AI powered hiring" only to have the system crash during a critical client onboarding.

So, where do you start? First, take a long, hard look at your current HR tech stack. What's working, what's not, and where are the glaring gaps that AI can fill? Are your recruiters drowning in resumes, desperately searching for that diamond in the rough? Time to bring in the algorithmic cavalry with smart resume screening and filtering. Struggling to keep up with the sheer volume of candidate outreach? A chatbot concierge can handle the initial touchpoints, freeing your team to focus on the high value interactions.

But here's the kicker - don't just slap on the latest AI tool and call it a day. Integration is key. You want your AI solutions to work in perfect harmony, seamlessly passing the baton from one stage of the hiring process to the next. Imagine a well oiled machine, where predictive analytics identify top talent, automated interviews assess their skills, and intelligent onboarding ensures a smooth transition to the new role. It's a beautiful thing, like a perfectly choreographed dance recital, if the dancers were robots. And let's not forget the importance of good old fashioned human oversight - you need to maintain that delicate balance between technological wizardry and good old fashioned common sense.

Ensuring Reliable and Secure Infrastructure

Now, let's talk about the backbone of your robo recruiting platform - the infrastructure. This is where the rubber meets the road, folks. You can have the most cutting edge AI algorithms in the world, but if your system crashes during a critical hiring cycle, it's game over. And let's not even get started on the security implications - data breaches, unauthorized access, and all that other nightmarish stuff that keeps CIOs up at night.

First and foremost, invest in a vigorous and adjustable cloud infrastructure. We're talking redundancy, failover mechanisms, and the kind of elastic computing power that can handle those sudden spikes in candidate traffic. And don't forget about security - encryption, access controls, and rigorous data governance protocols. Because let's face it, when it comes to sensitive HR data, you don't want to be the agency that ends up on the front page of the tech blog for all the wrong reasons.

But infrastructure is more than just servers and security. It's also about smooth integrations with your existing HR software, smooth data flows, and the ability to quickly onboard new clients without breaking a sweat. Think of it like building a high performance sports car – you need the engine, the brakes, and the handling to all work in perfect harmony, or you're going to end up in a ditch. And trust me, you don't want to be the one explaining to your clients why their essential hiring campaign just hit a metaphorical tree.

Maintaining Agility and Continuous Improvement

Alright, let's talk about the secret sauce that separates the robo recruiting superstars from the also rans – agility and continuous improvement. Because in this fast paced, ever evolving world of talent acquisition, standing still is about as helpful as a chocolate teapot.

First and foremost, build a culture of innovation and experimentation. Encourage your team to think outside the box, to embrace the weird and wonderful ideas that might just be the next big thing. After all, who would have thought that a campaign featuring dancing avocados would be the key to revealing that elusive Millennial talent pool? (Spoiler alert: it was us, and it worked like a charm.)

But innovation without execution is just a nice idea – you need to put rubber to the road and constantly iterate on your robo recruiting platform. Regularly assess your AI models, test new features, and be willing to ruthlessly cut the things that aren't working. Because let's be honest, that cutting edge chatbot you implemented six months ago? It's probably already yesterday's news. Stay ahead of the curve, my friends, and you'll be the ones setting the trends, not just chasing them.

And let's not forget about the human element. Your team of HR experts and tech wizards are the backbone of your robo recruiting success. Invest in their continuous learning, allow them to experiment, and create an environment where failure is seen as an opportunity, not a four letter word. Because let's face it, the day you stop learning is the day you become irrelevant. And in this industry, irrelevance is the kiss of death.

The Future of Robo Recruiting

Emerging Trends and Innovations in AI for HR

Fasten your seatbelts, folks, because the world of robo recruiting is about to get a whole lot more, well, robotic. As we peer into the crystal ball of HR tech, one thing is clear: the future is bursting with mind blowing advancements that will redefine the way we find, assess, and manage talent. Prepare to be amazed, because the next generation of AI powered HR solutions is about to turn the recruitment industry on its head.

First up, let's talk about the rise of the "super recruiter" - an AI assistant so intelligent and versatile, it'll make your head spin. Imagine a virtual headhunter that can scour the depths of the internet, identifying top tier candidates with laser like precision, all while navigating the complexities of candidate engagement, interview scheduling, and even employment negotiations. This AI powered Sherlock Holmes of the HR world will be your secret weapon, scouting out the elusive passive candidates that traditional methods just can't reach.

But that's just the tip of the iceberg. As AI continues to evolve, we're about to witness the emergence of "hyper personalized" recruiting experiences that will make candidates feel like they're the only person on the planet. Imagine a world where every interaction, from the job description to the onboarding process, is tailored to the individual's unique needs, preferences, and aspirations. It's like having a personal concierge for your hiring journey – and trust me, top talent is going to eat it up.

And let's not forget about the power of predictive analytics. In the not so-distant future, your robo recruiting platform will be able to forecast hiring trends, identify skills gaps, and even pinpoint the next superstar employees – all before they even cross your radar. Imagine the competitive edge you'll have when you can proactively build a pipeline of qualified candidates, ready to pounce on the next big opportunity.

Preparing for the Workforce of Tomorrow

As if the current situation of robo recruiting wasn't futuristic enough, buckle up for the seismic shifts that are about to reshape the very nature of work. We're talking about a workforce that's more fluid, more diverse, and more tech savvy than ever before, and your robo recruiting strategy needs to be ready to adapt.

Gone are the days of the traditional 9 to-5 grind. The workforce of the future is all about flexibility, remote work, and the rise of the gig economy. Your robo recruiting platform will need to be adaptable enough to source, screen, and manage a constantly evolving pool of talent – from freelancers and contractors to full time employees and everything in between.

And the diversity factor? Hold on to your hats, because it's about to get real. The next generation of workers will be more globally connected, more culturally diverse, and more tech savvy than ever before. Your robo recruiting tools will need to be equipped to navigate this kaleidoscopic talent terrain, ensuring that your hiring process is inclusive, bias free, and open to the boundless possibilities that this diverse workforce has to offer.

But it's not just about the candidates – your own HR team will need to evolve as well. Get ready for the rise of the "AI fluent" HR professional, a breed of HR experts who can seamlessly blend human expertise with cutting edge technology. These HR ninjas will be the ones who can employ the full power of robo recruiting tools, interpret the observations, and translate them into strategic, people centric solutions that drive business success.

Envisioning the Next Generation of Talent Acquisition

Alright, buckle up, because we're about to dive headfirst into the wild and wonderful world of the future of talent acquisition. It's going to be a wild ride, so make sure you've got your seatbelt securely fastened and your imagination cranked up to 11.

First and foremost, get ready for the rise of the "talent concierge" – a hyper personalized, AI powered assistant that will guide candidates through every step of the hiring process. Imagine a virtual wingman that can anticipate your needs, tailor the experience to your unique preferences, and even negotiate on your behalf. It's like having a personal shopper for your dream job, and trust me, top talent is going to be lining up to work with these futuristic headhunters.

But the real game changer is the way this next gen talent acquisition will make use of the power of immersive experiences. Forget boring old video interviews and standardized assessments – the future is all about gamification, virtual reality, and even augmented reality. Imagine stepping into a virtual office, interacting with holographic colleagues, and completing challenges that truly showcase your skills and potential. It's like a high stakes, high tech version of the Crystal Maze, and the candidates who excel will be the ones who land the job.

And let's not forget about the role of predictive analytics in shaping the future of talent acquisition. Imagine a world where your robo recruiting platform can not only identify top talent, but also predict their future performance, potential for growth, and even their likelihood of staying with the company long term. It's like having a crystal ball for your hiring decisions, and it's going to remake the way we think about talent management.

So there you have it, folks – a glimpse into the not so-distant future of robo recruiting. Hold on tight, because the next few years are going to be a wild ride, full of mind blowing innovations, game changing technologies, and a whole lot of robotic goodness. But one thing's for sure: the future of talent acquisition is bright, and it's going to be a heck of a lot of fun.

Silas Meadowlark

www.ingramcontent.com/pod-product-compliance
Lightning Source LLC
Chambersburg PA
CBHW030505220526
45464CB00006B/2662